From Spires to Peaks

A collection of poetry by Anthony L. T. Cragg

This book is dedicated to my three most inspirational teachers:

Christopher Stuart-Clark

Jeremy Lemmon

Professor Christopher Butler

Contents

Introduction

When I was a small boy, if anyone asked me what I wanted to be when I grew up, I gave one of two answers. Usually, to amuse the adults, I would say "bartender", but sometimes I would tell them the truth; that I wanted to be a poet. It wasn't until my early teens that I discovered, for reasons largely incomprehensible to my youthful, romantic brain, being a poet wasn't considered a "real" job at all.

So, when the time came to look for work, I decided instead to choose fields that I could just about convince myself were 'writing adjacent'.

The first of these was teaching, demanding enough in itself, even more so on the other side of the world. At the venerable age of 22, and straight out of university myself, I started teaching English at a university in Japan. My girlfriend bravely agreed to join me there and, a couple of years later, even more bravely, agreed to be my wife. Together, we struggled to come to grips with the language and culture of Japan, both challenging and captivating in equal parts. We will always treasure the memory of those 'Nihon-jin' who took pity on two young strangers in a "strange" land. Some of them remain dear friends to this day.

As much as we came to love Japan, I am sure my students would agree that teaching was not my natural calling and after two extraordinary years, we returned to England. There I decided that journalism might be the answer to my career angst. For my second attempt at a job that was both real and involved writing, I got a position as the Assistant Editor of a magazine. Inevitably, it took less than a year to realise that, while being paid to write was all well and good, there were two problems with the job. One was the not inconsiderable problem that the main subject matter of the magazine was of no interest to me. The other was that, while the job did come with a new, rather cute Renault Clio, it came with a salary which was barely enough to keep body and soul together. I was in what seemed the worst of both worlds, not writing what I wanted, but not getting paid enough to write what I didn't want to.

Clearly, writing for other people wasn't going to work for me. I was confronted with a stark choice between trying to make a living out of writing for myself, in which case I would probably starve, or making a living in some other way, while writing, for myself, on the side. To some it might seem cowardly, to others sensible, but I chose what seemed to me the safer option and ended up in the world of international investment. I consoled myself at the time that I wasn't so much selling my soul to the devil as renting it for a while. As it turned out, what was intended to be a brief fling with Mammon turned out to be a long, love-hate relationship from which it took me years to extricate myself.

Throughout four different jobs in five different countries around the world, there were always two constants that sustained me. One was my lovely, loving wife and the other my poetry. Having started writing poems when I was sent away to boarding school at the age of seven, I have never stopped doing so, at least intermittently, ever since. Whatever my daily occupation, I always considered myself a poet. I began to think of it as a blessing rather than a compromise that I could write what I wanted without the pressure of having to make a living from it.

The wanderlust that had driven us to leave England and to spend years living around Asia, eventually led us to make our home high up on a mountain in Colorado. With a few earlier exceptions, this is a collection of fifty poems composed on that long and winding journey from the dreaming spires to the Rocky Mountains.

Quiet, Please!

He cannot see the singer strut and stroll.
He cannot hear the blues or rock 'n roll.
He's found a job to keep him off the dole.
We call it rent-a-thug. He calls it crowd control.

Even if he didn't earn a penny,
he'd be as happy as a sand-boy when he
stands with his clone-like cronies, feared by many.
His task is to keep the peace and he's not taking any.

His pose owes less to human than ideal.
Is he made of flesh and blood or hardened steel?
Does he breathe like you and me, and would he feel
my finger if I poked him? Is he real?

Except through his ears you cannot look through
this huge and sinister form in front of you,
though if he could talk he'd swear it's true
he's not specifically required to block your view.

Don't be deceived by his air of external calm.
Inside his head his master's set the alarm.
A warning pat from that bionic arm
is sometimes construed as grievous bodily harm.

continued...

At such a time, the slightest movement's barred:
to stand, to breathe, to tap your feet or, God
forbid, to dance. In fact, it's pretty hard
to see who guards the guarded from the guard.

(1974, London)

Wonder Drug

There's magic in it, powers of healing
not yet approved by the F.D.A.,
nor covered by your health plan.
Floods of tears and wails of pain
are instantly hushed by it.
No pill, no cream, no bandage works faster
to restore a child
to health and happiness.
It is a kind of benediction,
the nearest thing to a blessing
that the laity are capable of,
bestowing with one small movement of the lips
safety and solace. It equips
the recipient with all the protection
a parent can give
for college or parties or bicycle trips.
What is it? Of course,
it is a mother's kiss.

(March 3rd, 2000, Evergreen, Colorado)

Untimely Ripped

Feel my body melt,
each straining limb subside.
The love we both so strongly felt,
can leave no strength inside.

Not since I first was brought
kicking and struggling to my mother's lap
have I been so securely caught
in loving arms, or so completely trapped.

But out of my own free will, I mean.
I know that there's nowhere outside,
with no-one that I'd rather be.
Where safer than a prison could I hide?

Why should I leave this honoured place,
watching for every tender sign
that only a lover could find in your face,
that face too perfect to be mine?

I ought to go. It's getting late,
but since our hearts detest such pain,
dissolve, consume, evaporate,
take all of me so I need never leave again.

(1975, Oxford)

Early Flight

I leave you like a lover,
Colorado, as the aspens silver.
I leave you sparkling,
piercing the sight
with colours that are almost painful,
and, like a lover, long for you
even before I have left you.
There is no easy time to lose
the soothing sway of evergreens,
the terrible eloquence of stone,
but this perhaps is the hardest,
when all the lives of the mountain,
great and small, unbury themselves
from the oblivion of winter.
This is when each morning is an explosion of spring
and the early air as I walk through it
fractures into shards of sunlight.

(1999, Evergreen, Colorado)

For Diane

The world has grown a little older,
heaven, no doubt, a little louder
now that that great heart no longer beats.
Sometimes still I think I see her,
trailing clouds of fur behind her,
weaving her ancient bike through Mayfair streets.

It always seemed she had so much to give
she needed several lives to live,
inventor, politician, star of The West End.
She gave her all to every role
mind and body, heart and soul,
whether filling in a crossword or helping out a friend.

In person, famously attractive,
in intellect, tirelessly active,
Diane was born and lived and died a star.
No wonder fans from all those years
join with us now in smiles and tears.
So many loved her from afar.

Diane, I thank you for the life
of Claudia who became my wife.
What greater gift than an elder daughter?
But we are all forever in your debt
for all those things we should never forget
for memories of kindness, memories of laughter.

(2002, Charter Alley, Hampshire - Read at the funeral of Diane Hart)

All-American Girl

Miss Candy Screamer of Arizona,
with friend and admirer, Mr Bullwhip Dollar,
all in sleek, pink elegance
Cadillac'ed out of the bounds of Ma's good sense,
and only sometimes, briefly, at night repents.

Diamonds and sunglasses are enough
to cover the bruises when he treats her rough
or too much like a bit of expensive stuff.
Only once (when a cheque bounced) has she wept
and sleeps as only the innocent could have slept,
and keeps what she likes and likes being kept.

As for Bullwhip, he is kind and content
only when she makes him forget what he's spent
by paying him back in kind for his investment.
The end of this tale I am loath to impart,
as it is, I am afraid, somewhat sadder than the start.
One day, sweet Candy, with her legs apart,
in mid-scream quite literally broke his heart.

(1982, Hong Kong)

For Absent Friends

We do not lose them, we misplace them.
They are the victims of forgetful love.
They are dear and yet we can replace them,
close and yet not close enough.

As soon as they have helped us on our way
we shed them like old skin.
They are the necessary price to pay
for a new life to begin.

We say we'll write, we'll keep in touch,
we'll phone, we'll drop a line,
but the words we need to say so much
lie buried till the end of time.

They are quotations that we cannot quite recall,
fragments of songs no longer in style.
Could it be that they were never real at all,
just ghosts that came to haunt us for a while?

(2008, Evergreen, Colorado)

Long Weekend

On Monday night after you've gone,
it's always the same:
I feel the need
to embrace what's left of me.
We cannot cheat the evening.
It will return to claim
the tears we owe it from the day.
And time falls
in many mysterious ways,
even as we speak,
deluding me,
confusing with a thousand empty tasks.
The bell pursues me as I walk
the path that all mankind has taken.
Around me, avenues of hope
lead to doorways of hope,
lead to the thing itself;
an empty room.
Its sheer reality
drowns me,
and the life that you breathed into me
is on its way to Paddington.

(1975, Oxford)

Cityscape

I have been lucky enough to live
with views of snow-capped peaks and mountain lakes,
at other times of oceans, the blue Pacific and the grey South China Sea
or of soft, green English valleys and placid lawns.
But now, in refuge, our landscape is a narrow back alley,
lined with garage doors and utility poles
and brightened by the greens and blues
not of grass and water but of garbage bins.
No subject matter here for sure for Constable or Palmer
and Ansel Adams wouldn't need his camera to record what I can see.
Yet somehow in these strange and fearful times,
this prosaic spectacle of urban life
and of the simple everyday mechanics of human existence
seems safe and reassuring,
strangely appropriate and in its way,
entirely beautiful.

(April 26th, 2020, Calgary)

For Suzette

Your leaving left a void I cannot fill,
a wound that will not heal,
a tear that falls still.

Your not being here is with me every day,
your absence an uninvited guest
who will not go away.

You're over there, just over there, a breath away,
and yet the fare to take me there
is too high a price to pay.

(2008, Evergreen, Colorado)

Now and Forever

Don't ask me to explain, I beg you,
this that the city does to me,
this that at night can move me to the brink of tears
and beyond.
It is a strange and living thing
when all around is fretful
and the ragged people tear in fury at their ragged lives.
Somehow the air outside
tells of a Sunday evening
'though the curtains and the windows are closed.
And tomorrow is a Monday that I have to face alone
without your help,
when even the thought of you
is driven from my head
by all that endlessly is meant
to mean something to me
and never does.

(1973, Harrow)

Sunnyvale

"I saw to him, alright.

Oh yes, Sir, I saw to him.

Wouldn't give in at first,

kept muttering something about love and peace;

you know, all that stuff we had back in '68.

Well, I had another patient to attend to at the time,

calls himself 'John', won't give a second name.

Strange one that, got this thing about water,

can't keep him out of the fountain.

Anyway, I had to go and do something about him;

so I left this other one alone for a while.

Mind you, I knew he'd only go making a nuisance of himself,

laying his hands on people and things, the way he does.

So I made him sit down on one of the benches in the garden

thought it might do him a bit of good being in the sun a while.

Of course, I tied his wrists to the back of the bench

with a bit of rope I always carry on me.

But, here's the funny bit;

when I got back, his hands were tied alright, but not by rope.

There were bloody great nails sticking right through them.

I never was much good at tying knots.

'E must have got away to the tool shed

that some of our Class A patients are allowed to use.

continued...

Beats me, though, how he could have done both hands,

must have used his mouth I suppose.

I hear he was quite a carpenter in his time.

Still, I made him pay for it,

got him put in solitary. Oh yes, I saw to him, alright.

Couldn't have him disturbing the other patients like that.

There was one in particular who saw him

just sitting there bleeding, bleeding.

'Mary' I think her name was.

Right cut up about it she was, poor thing,

and such a nice girl too

(though, of course, I couldn't speak for her past).

Cried for weeks afterwards, she did.

Couldn't console her,

had to be sedated.

Terrible how she cried."

(1983, Hong Kong)

Inside Voice

Said my spirit to my body:
I am tired of being constrained
in a twenty-two square foot tiny home of skin,
cluttered with two hundred pounds
of flesh and bone and muscle,
while I am as light as nothing
and as large as everything.
I am bored by your constant need
to sleep and eat and defecate,
by your hunger and your thirst
and your aches and pains,
while I am pure energy
and fed by a higher purpose.
I know you can run and swim, but I can fly
over the mountaintops or across the Milky Way.
Yet even so I will stay with you,
for as long as your home is full of music
and your heart is full of love.

(August 15th, 2020, Gulf Islands, British Columbia)

I.P.O. [OMG]

It's hard now to recall a time
[before the internet existed]
when companies before they listed
had to show a bottom line.

Today it couldn't matter less
nor do we let it now affect us
if, looking through a stock's prospectus,
we find no hint of EPS.

On this new investment scene
requiring earnings seems absurd.
If 'profit' is a dirty word,
these IPOs are squeaky clean.

Just flip your way out of money troubles.
Cash is the coward's place to hide.
Investment banks have never lied
so let's have no more talk of bubbles.

Buy today while you still can
with every dollar you can borrow,
then sell the sucker hard tomorrow
and go to work in earnest – on your tan.

(2014, Singapore)

Mistical Morning

From the sea below
a chill, grey mist slides up the hill towards us
like a ghostly lover,
caressing the fields, kissing the trees.
Only now it is near does its mood darken,
subtly congealing to a glutinous fog
that seems to have devoured the whole known world
right up to the edge of our curtilage.
There it masses like an invading army,
ready to lay siege.

(October 9th, 2020, Gulf Islands, British Columbia)

For Lily

I always trusted words.

They used to be relied on

for comfort and relief,

but now they seem

no more than what they are,

black scratchings on a sea of white,

too thin and insubstantial to support

the burden of such grief.

James and Sarah,

even in my darkest nightmare I can barely guess

the bitter pain of your loss.

But though Lily has left us,

a single white flower,

cut down so cruelly on a dark Dublin street,

she will be with you every day,

not, as now, as a source of sorrow,

but as a loving and companion spirit,

set free from the limitations of this physical form,

behind which our true selves so often hide,

to be, despite her young years, a pure, old soul,

a constant comfort to you

and a guide.

continued...

So we must still use words, must talk, must live,
though those who were nearest to us
suddenly seem, at first, so distant.
I myself have spoken every day of my life
to a father I never knew,
so how much more real to you
will Lily be,
whose voice you can still recall,
whose grace and beauty you can still see
in your mind's eye,
whose smiling face still shines
so brightly in your memory?

And Charlotte, you are now
closer to Lily than you have ever been,
because your senses are now her senses too.
She will hear through your ears
a surge of music or a baby's gurgle,
see through your eyes a rolling sea
or light refracted through a stand of trees.
Through your skin she will feel
a dog's rough fur
or the gentle stroking of a summer breeze.

(April 22nd, 2007, Evergreen, Colorado)

Questions

How can you calmly sleep so far away?

Say in the night I wake and need you,

how then could you save me?

For I have searched and kept my eyes so wide

they hurt with staring. Still I see

no other place in all the world, no room for me.

I strained that you might gently take my hand.

I cried that you might smile.

I paid my dues in love a thousand times to find

all that I prize, yes, even you,

as mortal as I.

This morning, was I not born again,

and did I not call your face

and the rising sun the same?

This evening, was I not reduced to 'Whatsizzname'

and am I not dead?

Except, no tomb could be as cold

as this my bed.

(1974, Oxford)

Tokyo Calling

I feel your love
leap like an electric spark
across the many thousand miles between us,
recharging me with all the energy
I never have without you.
I see it fly
over the endless tundra of Siberia,
swoop low over this city and alight
panting but triumphant on my windowsill.
I know it to be mine,
for me alone,
and with a thousand magic words of love
no other heart could know,
it gains admittance to my room.

(1978, Tokyo)

4952 Aspen Drive

Here on the corner of this dusty mountain street,
I have proudly stood for forty years.
My walls have battled wind and snow and sleet,
but are no match for children's tears.

I wasn't designed or built to be alone,
but the family I sheltered have gone for good.
I am nothing if I am not a home,
just a pile of glass and nails and wood.

Outside, the garden toys are still in place.
Basketball hoop and swing, trampoline and slide
portray to the neighbours my happy family face
and reveal no hint of the emptiness inside.

Inside, I am as dark and still and quiet as a tomb,
devoid of light and sound and life.
Love is no longer made in the master bedroom
since the great divide between man and wife.

Where is my dog who loved to bark and run
and my kids who loved to squeal and play?
I am a land-locked ghost-ship now that they are gone
and I myself have had my day.

continued…

Even my builder cannot tell me when to die.
I cannot wait until my walls fall down.
Maybe the next time lightning stalks the sky
I'll let it strike and burn me to the ground.

Now that I have witnessed with my own wooden eyes
the mutually assured destruction of divorce,
there's nothing in nature, now I realise,
no storm, no disaster of such cruel force.

(September 26th, 2019, Evergreen, Colorado)

Autumn

Now it is autumn,
and the sweat of lovers
lying in the fields
is confused by rain.
Now the long, cold hardness of the sea
is undisturbed by a single flailing limb,
its silence unbroken by a single frivolous laugh.
Instead, overhead sea birds fly
who, though this winter seem sure to die,
expect no epitaph.
Again, questions one simply does not ask,
are asked,
having never been answered;
and songs that have haunted since childhood
return unwanted, unrecalled
with a sniff of winter.

(1972, Harrow)

Sleeping Beauty

When,
crumpled with tiredness,
I come back to you,
all curled and full of sleep,
then I will tell you
how a unicorn
caught by its single horn
is a rare thing,
but will not run away.
Only watch
the roaring anarchy of the sea
(its terrible pointless fury)
with a humble heart,
and you will see perhaps its subtle innocence,
remember how we played with the waves
and how they played with us.
And so your limbs,
though sunk into the white amorphous sheets,
retain
their own astonishing power
and I am hesitant to touch them,
wary of what I do not understand,
frightened lest I thus unleash
forces of love not even a lover could stand.

(1976, Oxford)

Escape from the City

Even on a cold, hard, dirty London street,
may soft, green sod stretch out beneath your feet.
May all the frantic shoppers and commuters
turn into foxes and squirrels, larks and butterflies,
and the garish colours of advertising hoardings and shopping bags
mellow into the subtle hues of nature.
May the chatter of the crowd and the harsh drone of traffic
become the joyful chirps and trills of birdsong,
and the acrid smell of car fumes
the fresh, sweet scent of wildflowers.
And may the gentle sun warm your upturned face
as you stroll, now entirely alone,
through the lush meadows of Oxford Street.

(December 1st, 2019, Evergreen, Colorado)

Presentation

Buttons are strained by the urging of pride.

Stomachs are too prominent themselves through years of surfeit.

Like a line of robins, pompous and over-red

through years of drink and sedentary power,

though never, of course, would they think to wipe away

the sweat beneath their freshly laundered collars

lest they appear

susceptible to bodily functions.

There they stand, in the glow of serried, staring admiration

from the people beyond.

You'd never think they move or could do so,

but when the time has come

for the lily-white glove to touch their flesh,

every limb is tendentious,

every whisper inspired,

and they are left

empty but edified

as she passes along.

(1986, London)

To Sister Moon [with Apologies to Francis of Assisi]

Your brother, the Sun,
dazzles in such an obvious way,
blazing down on beaches
and bursting through the clouds.
We know, we know
without him we freeze to death
and nothing grows.
We are never allowed to forget
our absolute dependence
and cannot even look directly at his face.
We rarely speak about the dark side of the Sun.
When he forgets his own strength,
he blinds what he means to brighten
and what he means to warm, incinerates.
This giver of life has his death rays, too.
Whether the sun is friendly or fierce,
he still must set and yield the world to you,
Sister Moon, the Queen of the Night.
You are our friend among the stars
and do no harm.
We don't need moonshades or moonscreen
and there's no such thing as moonburn.

continued…

Your strength is measured,

your light modest and refined.

Your gift is to illuminate

not always what we see,

but what we think and feel most deeply.

You shine as much within us as around us.

Without the sun, we cannot live

but, without the moon,

perhaps we wouldn't want to.

(December 5th, 2020, Gulf Islands, British Columbia)

The Streets of San Francisco

I see her from a window table
of a restaurant on Fourth Street,
a lady not as old perhaps as life has made her,
but far too old to be living rough.
Weighed down by a sack of her possessions
almost bigger than she is,
she is walking, but it's more like she is climbing up the slope,
as though at any moment
she may have to use her hands as well.
Bent over into the cold headwind
her body itself has formed a question mark,
begging answers.
From behind and from in front of her,
passers-by pass by,
some almost colliding with her,
seemingly unaware of her existence,
and I wonder for a second if only I can see her,
if my own guilty mind has created the image of her…
but she is real enough, all too real.
Her fine grey hair streams out behind her in the breeze,
so much like my own mother's used to do.

continued…

I watch each painful step she takes
until she slowly fades from view
and even then I cannot look away
from the grey, unforgiving street,
almost hypnotised by the sadness of the scene.
And then, unnoticed, the waiter appears
and then, unwanted now, the food is served
and then, unbidden, the tears come.

(2015, San Francisco)

Night Duty

I wonder what the moon pretends
behind that solitary face it shows.
On nights like this, my waiting ends
and the night is all I know.

The trees can't hide me, try as they might,
stretching their fingers through the yellow light.
Like an old, bald judge, its moral admonitions
pour on my head so cold, with so many conditions.

Lord, let me drown
in the murky waters of the deep,
so the nightmare men who walk around
will see I am asleep
and keep their terrors to themselves.

Lord, will my bed leave the ground
with no noise,
leaving nothing of this life you gave me,
more dream than reality
till I hear your voice?

(1970, Harrow)

Renaissance

I drown in moonlight,
I, who couldn't sleep,
out of bed, feet cold,
sitting by the window.
Like a drowning man,
see my life before me,
but, because it is night,
a life I never led,
things I never said
to people long since dead.
And yet I rejoice
in all such scenes.
Because I am who I am,
I rejoice in what I never did,
and wake in the morning
a new man.

(1971, Harrow)

Fait Accompli

And on the beach when the joy is done,
let the waters come
and carry us away.
We cannot live when once our time has come
and angels flee
in panic from the day-to-day.

We shall not see,
if so you talk and squat,
the waves roll in and break upon the shore,
reminding us in subtle watery ways of what
we were and what we are no more.

They cannot walk on gravel roads
whose feet have grown accustomed
to the supple warmth of sand.

(1972, Harrow)

Pearls That I Have Trampled Under Trotter

Were I to sit alone
these last few hours,
betray what faith in ourselves we have come to know,
squander what love we have dared to call ours,
were I to do this one momentous thing,
it would be more or less atonement
for all the hours I muttered when my heart would sing
for very love of God and you and the joy that you both have meant.

Surely this is a kind of hell I feel:
scrutinised by faces that I do not want to see,
cornered into truths I do not want to know,
leaving what I do not want to leave,
going where I do not want to go.

So whole, so perfect in its simple beauty,
your face was luminous with other than a human light.
The curve of your cheek, the mist in your eyes meant more to me
than prayed-for guarantees of my survival through a sleepless night.

Contrary still in what now seems the last extreme,
I must untie these last few threads that hold you down.
For whoever saw a beggar kiss a queen
and who wouldn't kill a moth inside a ballroom-gown?

(Michaelmas Term 1976, Oxford)

Dusk in The Rockies

Across the valley houses reveal themselves
as darkness falls,
every light a life or several lives
on the mountains' side.
Each shows what Auden called an affirming flame,
burning brightly,
hundreds of tiny acts of human defiance
against the night.

(February 8th, 2020, Evergreen, Colorado)

Wanted: Dead or Dead

"There are no heroes in crime".

So "Justice" is served. Society's will is done.
Twenty submachine-gun shots erased
France's Public Enemy Number One.

Never before so graphically seen
a man is guilty till proven innocent
and no-one more guilty than Jacques Mesrine.

No clichés please about this savage trap,
no "Fair cop, guv". Not even he who was called
a second Dillinger could beat this rap.

On a busy Paris street, fifty gendarmes
waited in ambush to administer the law
and exercise it's long and dangerous arm.

Of special safety features there's no lack
in a BMW saloon, but no designer plans
against massive police attack.

Jacques' girlfriend, Sylvie Jeanjacquot,
was his passenger to the end but now he's left
for a place that she was lucky not to go.

And if her parents do not sue, I pray
the poodle on her lap whose death spared hers
will be avenged by the French SPCA.

continued…

Policemen grinned in triumph when he died
and armchair hunters by their TVs hailed
each calculated wound in the monster's hide.

The morning papers used his blood for ink.
Lest any doubts assailed the people's minds
respected editors told them what to think.

A "filthy Commie rag" the only one
that failed to see the glory in the deed
and stubbornly refused to join the fun.

We must abide, as Shakespeare said,
our going hence as our coming hither.
Still one can but wish a few tears shed.

Even if he had been speeding, it would be rough
to skip the fine and kill him there and then.
As if the Paris traffic wasn't bad enough.

(November 1979, Nagoya)

Birthday Poem

We always pretended we were two,
that I was I, and you were you.
We fooled the world that it was true
but always, deep inside, we knew
that we were never meant to be
divided into you and me
but, instead, one entity
united for eternity.

(September 27th, 2019, Evergreen, Colorado)

An Evening Walk with the Dogs

The cold is cruel,
as though the air itself was trying to hurt you.
The dogs watch and sniff and listen, alive to any threats,
except the virus they can neither see, nor smell, nor hear.

I look for answers
from the wise old moon
but it hides its yellow face behind a jagged row of rooftops.
Perhaps tonight it has no answers.

In the gathering gloom I search instead for a single star
and there at last I find one,
small and weak and watery,
but it's enough.

(April 5th, 2020, Calgary)

Breakfast at The Hallmark

Sadness clings to them
like the faint, musty smell of age and neglect.
Shuffling, heads bowed, what once were men and women
now strangely sexless
as when in infancy there are no such
arbitrary distinctions between us.
Now all alike are reduced to this,
the ultimate minimalism,
when merely being alive is at once enough
and too much.
Too quiet, too slow to be called a feeding frenzy,
yet they seem so purposeful in their quest
for porridge and grapefruit, muffins and prunes
and decaf coffee.
Some sit permanently smiling,
happy it seems at the re-occurrence of daylight
which streams through the skylight, bathing the scene
in a warm, serene glow,
creating in the dining room a little piece of heaven.

continued…

Others are sullen, scowling. Angry at what?

At the frailties of others that mock their own?

Or at the re-occurrence of daylight

which streams through the skylight, bathing the scene,

in a warm, serene glow,

creating in the dining room a little piece of heaven,

a little prematurely.

(1999, Chicago)

Classical Upbringing

They told me, by Calymachus,

that you were dead my son.

But now Cyrene's green-lined home

receives you with its chair of moss,

and table-shell still slimy from the parted waters.

My Aristaeus, what are you to me?

You come with querulous face,

begging answer to another's questions.

My heart grows weary

and my lungs too full of air.

Beg to leave me with my virgin and my newly-bearing nymphs;

sweet Arethusa, first to raise her head to you,

or young Lycorias with hair of gold.

Here I must remain

in myth and in the company of watery friends,

while Aristaeus leaves on Virgil's train

and unrequited is a mother's love.

(1972, Harrow)

A Thousand Thanks

If I had a thousand voices,
I could not tell
how often you've saved me.
If I had a thousand pens,
I could not put into words
how much you've made me.
Even with a thousand eyes
I could not see more clearly
who I'm living for,
and even with a thousand hearts
I could not love you more.

(May 28th, 2019, Evergreen, Colorado)

Rocky Mountains, Hi!

One thousand feet above a frozen lake,
where skaters' blades
carve trusting circles in the ice
and hardy, mufflered fishermen
carve all the way through,
a mile and a half above the sea
we have found a place.

High in the mountains,
where squirrels are as skittish
as foxes are fearless,
where rattlesnake refuse to climb
and mountain lion are rumoured to roam,
deep in the heart of The Rockies,
we have found a home.

Mount Evans to the North, Long's Peak to the East,
in this elevated state we can survey
the perfect pattern of our lives,
how we have come from there to there to here,
with barely a movement of the wheel
by our hesitant hands.

continued…

Through the clean, cold air

over the heads of the aspen trees,

we can more clearly see

how we were brought

against the laws of gravity,

against, almost, our own free will

"Nearer my God to Thee,"

to this peak,

to seek and find peace.

The air is hard to breathe,

its thinness that of life itself,

by whose silver thread

we hold our being

as precious and as vulnerable.

The moon tonight

is supernaturally bright,

casting down the slopes

its snow-reflected light,

and all below us fades into white,

leaving the world at last to you and me.

The town below is Evergreen;

so may our love be.

(December 1990, Evergreen, Colorado)

The Untouchables

Be still and let us lie like this
until the morning claims us.
Time and the night wash over,
but our bodies, once made warm,
shall never lose their heat again.
Strangers may stare benignly at us, call us lovers,
yet file us away with all the others.
We are not even of their flesh and blood,
whose flesh can ever cool, or blood run cold.
But we must leave
tomorrow till tomorrow.
Tonight, let us make
our love and take
what sleep we can.

(1974, Oxford)

Solo Voyage

I have drifted for hours alone
on the quiet ocean of the night
with nothing but a little raft of sleep
between me and the endless darkness.

(May 29th, 2019, Evergreen, Colorado)

For Andrew

It was by Skype that I last spoke to you.

>You recommended a book for me to read.

In an email from a mutual friend, I learnt that you had died.

>As soon as I saw the subject line, "Sad news", I knew.

On Instagram I sent my condolences to your daughter.

>She had posted a photo of you as you were when I first knew you.

Via a live video link, I watched your funeral

>and your coffin theatrically disappearing to who knows where.

I hold out hope that it is only in the new digital world that you are gone,

that in some old analog existence you and I still learn and laugh and drink.

It's past midnight,

but sleep and I are on different continents

and I am thinking of you

who now can neither sleep nor wake.

(December 19th, 2020, Gulf Islands, British Columbia)

Written After Seeing a Painting by Sisley of the River Thames

A day like this is a day believed for an instant, then forgotten.
How long will the sunlight fill my mind with its contentment?
And, how do I know that the sky that moves so slowly now,
will not in time turn red and pour recriminations on me for a wasted day?

Once before was a summer's day like this,
when the waters laughed at the rowers' idle energy,
and the earth held its hot eternity in a single day.
Once before did I imagine life was as it should be,
and that God smiled still on man in spite of his winter sadness.

Now, I find myself hoping again
that the long hours of darkness will leave my brain,
as I lie on my back on the yielding grass,
and the sun warms my cold hopes and my old illusions.

There is a boat down there where the willow weeps.
I could row across in an instant to the other side
where the happy people play with their picnics and their parasols,
and the flag as it flutters boasts of a nation's optimism.

continued...

But I rather think I will stay on this side,

and ruin my enjoyment by wondering

what the world will say tomorrow if the rain beats down.

Will the people say we didn't know, how could we know

that the iron bridge we so admired would bear our sense away

or that I should have told them love and joy were but passing things

like the patterns of the shadows on the water,

broken in the twinkling of an eye by a thrashing oar,

while the Thames looked on and said nothing,

having seen it all before.

(1979, Nagoya)

A Lawyer's Declaration

Notwithstandingallthathasgonebefore

I

contrarytotheopinionyoumayhaveofme

am

forthwithhenceforthandheretofore

in

onthesideofundertheinfluenceofuptomyneckin

love.

(1975, Oxford)

Heathrow, Deathrow

Suddenly appalled,
B.B.C. news,
six o'clock apathy,
after the pay disputes and the "disturbances"
by a brief report; the story of some fifty swans,
ordered from the Argentine by a Birmingham livestock firm.
Well, they're dead stock now, twenty-five of them at least.
Porters at Heathrow were alerted by the smell,
opened the crates and found them,
packed, I would say like sardines
but no sardine was ever packed alive.
My God, they would have stood a better chance
to fly themselves the several thousand miles
from the Pampas to the Bullring.
What smiling stewardess said to them
"We hope you enjoyed your flight"?
And now the R.S.P.C.A. move in
to bust this particular cygnet ring;
but the swans are dead.
Their lovely necks are folded back
on breasts perfectly still on the hot tarmac.

It is said swans sing before they die
but in the roaring belly of a giant metal bird
nobody heard their song.

(1971, Harrow)

Initial Love

Can I, or anyone, spell 'l-o-v-e'?
Letters alone are not enough.
Another form is now long overdue.
Unless the words themselves are true
Defining love in words will never do.
I only know of one that might explain:
A seven-letter woman's name.

(2012, Singapore)

Retired Hurt

Now that our daughters have escaped
the poor excuse of tears
and our sons have woken
all their sleeping senses up,
is it true that we two have outgrown
what was not, for us, childhood
but life?
Or is there yet time
for love among the bath-chairs,
for passion to flower
in orderly gardens,
in all the places where
it ordinarily would,
were we not told to die,
were we not too old
to believe in lies,
yet still too young
to speak the truth?

(1978, Nagoya)

Green with Envy

How does it feel to be a tree
to spend your life reaching for the sky,
leaves dripping from your fingers,
to stand against the wind
so gracefully defiant,
to bow and not to break?

What is it like
to spread your roots so deep,
to know that this is where you are
and where you'll stay,
yet grow a little every day
and even in death, live on
in many different forms?

If you could stand so still, so long,
proud to be alone
but proud to be a part
of a vast community of living things
then you would know what it is like
to be a tree.

(2005, Evergreen, Colorado)

To Miss B.

I could lose my fingers painlessly,
running them for hours through your long black hair.
My nose I have no further need of,
now that it is filled with your sweet scent,
and where better could my own eyes drown
than in the deep dark pools of yours?
Trusting, clever, loving, and sweet,
in many ways you would make the perfect wife.
But the law I'm afraid pretty clearly prevents me
not only from committing bigamy
but from marrying my dog.

(2016, Evergreen, Colorado)

They Also Dream

Gasps and heavy breathing shake the bed.
No, not the first line of some erotic scene
but that most fragile and mysterious thing,
a dog's dream.

I'll never know what terrors roil his little body,
or what adventures make him run in his sleep
but when his squeals and pants become too alarming,
I only have to lay a hand on his heaving chest
and with one, long, cathartic sigh,
he is still again.

(September 6th, 2020, Gulf Islands, British Columbia)

40th Anniversary Poem

I'll never leave this honoured place,
watching for every tender sign
that only a lover can find in your face,
that face too perfect to be mine

(1981, London)

Whether we travel near and far
or choose to never leave this spot,
home is anywhere you are
and exile is anywhere you are not.

(February 7th, 2021, Gulf Islands, British Columbia)

Raison d'Être

You are the be-all and end-all
of all my being,
until all my being ends.

You are the beginning and end
of all that
under the sun I would defend.

You make me be all,
or at least end all
uncertainty as to what being to refuse.

You are Alpha and Omega
or any of the other
unnecessary conceits that poets choose.

(1988, Ashford Hill, Berkshire)

Acknowledgements

I would like to thank my wife and children for their help in compiling this collection. I would especially like to thank my daughter Cleo for her invaluable work in formatting, editing, and designing this book.

Index of Titles

About the Author

Anthony Louis Talbot Cragg was born in London in 1956 to Suzette and Wing Commander F. T. (Tim) Cragg. He attended school at Harrow and university at Christ Church, Oxford, where he read English Language and Literature. After graduating with a Master of Arts degree, he lived in both Asia and England for the next sixteen years before moving to the US in 1993. Having been a pioneer in several Asian stock-markets, he ended his financial career as the senior international fund manager at a major American bank. He and his wife Claudia now divide their time between Colorado, Canada, and the Cotswolds. They have three children, Adam, Toby, and Cleo, born respectively in Japan, England, and the US, and one grandchild, Astrid, born in Canada.

Previous Publications

"Pearls That I Have Trampled Under Trotter and Other Poems", Published in 1991 by Five Meadows Publishing, ISBN 0-9517223-0-1

"Poems 1970-2019", published in 2011 by Lulu, ISBN 978-1-257-05149-6